Pocket Sales Training Guide

Create a Sales Culture in 5 minutes

Whether you're leading sales in a retail big box environment or in a quick-serve restaurant, there are key tips to driving sales through trainable behaviors. If you don't take time to invest in your staff you won't see sales growth, it's as simple as that.

Book Sections:

Time Investment

Credentials

The Heart of the Matter

People Make the Difference

Case Study

Limited Options

Full Time versus Part Time

Shift Preference

Set Clear Expectations

One-on-One training

New Hires

Training 1: Average Ticket

Training 2: Consumer Confidence

Training 3: Asking the Right Questions

Training 4: Gross Margin

Cashiers

Closing

Time Investment:

If you're serious about creating a sales culture in your establishment you've got to be serious about investing in your employees. This doesn't mean taking hours every week to drill the same boring information down your employees throats, but it does mean *purposefully engaging your staff with the goal of change.* I try to focus on short 5 minute themes that you can share with your teams at the start of a shift. If you aren't starting your shift with a quick 1-2 minute team briefing, you're hurting your process.

Credentials:

The first thing we should discuss is why you want to listen to these guidelines in the first place.

Here's a little about my background, this isn't a pat on the back, rather showing that I'm brining useful tools from the real world.

OfficeMax Inc.: Sales Specialist, Technical Liaison, ASM Sales Manager

Amerisource Bergen Pharmaceuticals Operations Manager - Distribution Center Management

Sprint Nextel: Retention Specialist, Quality Analyst within the Data and Analytics Department, Advanced Technical Support

Hume Lake Christian Camps - Food Service Coordinator

Hartland Christian Camp - Food Service Director

The Heart of the Matter

You've likely heard it before, but customers are key to your sales. Over the years there have been psychological studies into the behaviors of consumers and many big box retailers subscribe to the fundamental principles of these studies. Through each organization I've worked with I have learned basic strategies for bringing up profits and reducing overhead costs. We'll explore these below.

People Make the Difference.

This is a basic concept that really rings true. I've made the mistake of keeping people on the sales team who simply couldn't sell early on in my career and my establishment and I suffered for it. Don't make this mistake. <u>Ultimately YOU are responsible for your sales culture and nice people that don't know how to sell won't get it done for you</u>. They may be nice people, they may have great qualities in other areas like attendance, but the fundamental issue is that unless you have the right person, you will never see the results you need.

Now, there are two main reasons that I've found that people are not the sales individuals that you need. The first is that they are not willing to be that person. The second is that they do not have the proper skills to be that person.

These are two serious differences. An employee not willing to try your strategies or follow your trainings or engage your customer is one that is apathetic. They will not be motivated and you must usher them out the door as soon as you can. Hire their replacement today.

An employee that does not have the skill to do the job has hope. The great thing about an employee without any skills is that you can train them specifically to your sales environment. Each time they learn something new and use it they become more and more valuable to your overall operation. They must be willing to learn, and often they are the most eager to learn because they know that they do not have a skill. These are my favorite employees. With some investment they will become your best performers and will remain loyal to your organization.

Case Study

This is a real life example. I had an employee that complained about his wages asking me if I expected him to take the job seriously at such low pay. By the way, at the time, the pay was $1/hr above minimum wage and he was only a 12-15 hour per week college student. I spoke with him for a few minutes and end the end made the following deal. I would give him a $.25/hr raise and he would improve his selling skills to appropriate levels within 30 days. He balked at the rate increase and I stated this was the first stage, if he really improved his performance not only would he be eligible for more hours but that I would be willing to look at his pay after another 90 days of performance. Against my better judgment I gave the small pay increase with expected results. His attitude didn't change, he didn't work any harder, but one thing did happen. After 30 days, he never complained about his pay again because he understood it was based on his efforts and he knew he wasn't meeting expectations. He left shortly thereafter.

The lesson: extra money didn't improve his performance. His basic issue was apathy and he was never going to become the sales person that I needed him to be. He naturally progressed out of position on his own, but at what cost? What would my quarterly results have been like had I hired a new employee sooner?

Limited Options

Let's face it, not everyone has a spiff or commission sales program, even those that do don't always make sense. Somehow at a big box retailer I was supposed to motivate my sales staff to sell key items like insurance for a spiff of a few pennies. Bottom line, I did not motivate my staff successfully this way and every moment I tried was a wasted opportunity for real and useful training for my staff. Follow your company guidelines and training, it's part of your job to be on board with corporate. Don't simply think this will work. You've got to go beyond this if you want real change.

So great, we spoke about what options we don't have. What about options we do have. Here are some creative ways to use the tools that you do have to manage your sales team.

First, total hours. You may be limited here, but you may not. At one location we had a cap of 24 hrs/week for part timers and a minimum of 9 hours to stay employed. I successfully used these guidelines to foster a sales environment. When I hired a new part time staff member I let them know I was going to work them about 12-15 hrs a week on average with more or less based on performance. I also let them know that they had a few weeks to get acclimated where they would be trained and given an opportunity to learn the skills needed to succeed before their hours were updated. This was a great tool.

Many sales managers are graded on key metrics such as total sales dollars, gross margin, add-ons, targeted promotions, and loyalty programs. If you're not your own boss, find out what you're being measured against. Hitting your numbers is key to remaining employed. You have to find out what numbers are the most important to your organization. Ours was focused on average ticket, gross margin, insurance, and loyalty subscriptions. For those not familiar I'll quickly cover what these key metrics are. Average ticket is simply the total amount of money the average customer spends. So say 10 customers represented $250 in sales that hour. So your average ticket was $250/10 = $25 per customer. This is a great average ticket. Many locations chase an average ticket of around $10 per customer. Gross Margin simply represents your profit after cost. So let's say you sell a $100 printer. That printer cost your store $95, and you sold it for $100 without any coupons or discounts. This means you made a gross margin of $5 ($100-$95=$5). This number is often represented as a percentage in a sales report. So

$5 is 5% of the $100, meaning your gross margin for that sale was 5%.

Full Time versus Part Time

Another tool you have is controlling your employee types. Your Full Time Employee positions are limited, likely you're forced to work with mostly part time individuals. You can reward part timers who excel by promoting them to Full Time when a position opens. Not everyone has this option. If you don't, then continue to reward your high performers with more hours, even if they just get 2-4 more hours per week, it does help. The more time your key employees are present, the more quality sales you'll get.

Shift Preference:

Let's face it, you should know when your sales are taking place. If you don't know the busiest times of your sales day, look it up now, or ask your data team to figure it out. Many POS systems have an hourly report option, look at it over a 12 month period. This tells you on average when your busiest times are. Reports are your friends, don't be afraid of them, learn how to read them. Once you know your key sales times, plan your sales force around them. You want your key individuals present when the majority of your sales occur. You'll see an increase in sales and margin when you have real sellers in the environment. It would be a waste to have a key sales person working during your down times. Find out what shifts employees like, and based on their performance work to more closely alight their schedule to those times whenever possible. A happy performer is going to perform even more for you.

Set Clear Expectations:

Not everyone is going to perform exactly the same way, it's just a simple fact, and no amount of training can really manipulate that. You can take a nonperformer and turn them into a performer but there are those that have more natural abilities than others. Reward progress. If your employee sold 1 insurance item the week before and this week they sold two, it's a big deal! That's a 100% increase in a week. Don't undervalue that improvement even though another employee gets 3-4 per week. They might get there as well, but it will take some time. Let your team know their daily, weekly, and monthly goals. This is why I can't stress the importance of a 1-3 minute start of the day sales huddle. You can call them out by name. "Joe, you need to get 2 insurance add-ons today, alright? I'm here to help, let's do this", "Sally, you're doing great on insurance, keep it up, but I'd really like to see you selling more paper with printers." etc. Let your team know the daily goal, is it 10 insurance add-ons for the day? Let them know, and push them to get there. Let them know your sales goal for the day, is it $14,000? Do you have 7 sales members that day? If they're all working the same total hours they should all work to personally sell $2,000 that day. Goals can be calculated with limited effort, know them well.

One-on-One training:

If you don't train individuals you won't get individual results. Often I see team trainings where the thought is the shotgun mentality. If you simply throw it at the whole team maybe some of them will remember or use it. While some trainings could benefit from a team environment, I haven't found that skill-specific training works well in this arena. Here's an example. You're telling your crew that you now sell a new type of camera. This would be a great team meeting or training. If you want your average ticket to go up, you'd invest your time more wisely if you trained one-on-one.

But you're busy, you don't have time for one-on-one training. I cannot stress this enough, you need to invest in training! BUT, here's the catch - you only have to train one person. I've found that part of reinforcing training is requiring your staff to teach each other. I've used this in sales and in food service. Take the time to train one employee- your best employee something. For average sales you could walk the store with your employee and talk about add-ons, or recommending higher dollar products. These are two simple ways to build your average ticket. Ask them questions, make them answer, make them role play briefly. In regards to role-playing, don't make it awkward. A team environment is very awkward and often they are more nervous in a group setting than they would be in a customer setting. Look at a printer with your employee and ask them what they could sell with it. A printer cable? Extra ink? Insurance? Next, tell them not to overwhelm a customer. Don't offer 5 add-ons. Pick one or two and leave it at that. Go over gross margin with them. Which of those add-ons produce the greatest profit for your store? The printer cable? That's what they should pitch. This is an example, you'll come up with your own ideas together, it's not that hard, just do it. So now you've invested 5-15 minutes on one employee. When your customer-base is slower have that employee take another employee through the same training you gave them. They'll put it in their own words, but you've effectively utilized other staff to train for you and you've reinforced that training in the original employee. Now both the first and second employee can train others. Ideally you'd want your best performers to do the training first and you'd want those performers to provide the training to others. Having a low performer train others is not what you want happening.

Later on you'll move to your next training, and you may need to spend 5-15 minutes with an employee now and again, you should plan to do this at least once a week. But that's it. You could, in theory, train your entire sales team with a 5 minute per week investment of your time. The more you do this, the faster the training will become. Your staff will gain an understanding of what the training is about and run with it. If your staff isn't running with it, it's time to hire new staff.

New Hires

New hires are your bread and butter. It's likely you came into position through a vacancy. Hopefully the person before you retired or got promoted, but let's face it, often in sales they didn't meet the criteria and were moved on. You may have inherited someone else's bad decisions but you don't have to live with them. I've seen defeated managers say they had no other options, you do have options, use them. I've already gone over how you can utilize hours to your advantage. If you have a team of 9 people, shaving 1 hour off of each means you now have 9 hours per week to hire a part time staff member. Obviously you don't want to rob from your top performers but this is just a simplified example. This will do two things. First, it will let your staff know you're serious. You haven't threatened anyone, that doesn't work, but you have let them know that they are getting less hours and you're looking to hire someone new. Sometimes this step alone changes the sales environment and you may end up not hiring anyone new because people finally understand and perform. Chances are you'll have one or two stragglers that don't get it and you'll dwindle their hours down or let them go to make room for a better sales staffer.

New hires represents fresh canvas for you to paint your views on. You can set clear expectations early on. Let them know that sales rules and hours will be given first to performers after their training time is complete. Drill into their minds early on that you have expectations that need to be met. It's easier to refer to this later on if they aren't performing. Communicate your needs to them. "I need someone who can increase each sale for every customer and offer our insurance." "Can you do that?" Then you're off to the right start. Don't rush the hiring process. Interview 1-3 individuals as soon as possible. If you don't see potential, don't hire them. Nothing prevents stacking a great sales team more than filling up your spots because you rushed the process. I understand you have needs, you have shifts to fill, you NEED that cashier yesterday. This book isn't about reacting to your day-to-day needs, it's about changing or creating a sales environment in your establishment. That's the only thing that will change your results. Over time you will have a sales team that you recruited, likely a blend of already existing staff with new behaviors and new hires that you've trained from the ground up.

Now that we've covered some basic managerial aspects of the sales culture, it's time to get into the quick trainings. Remember these work best on an individual basis. The quick 5 minute trainings are based on sales themes such as average ticket and will help your team meet those metrics.

Training 1: Average Ticket

Intro:

You cannot impact every customer purchase that comes through your door, but you can impact most.

The goal of today's training is to help you add value and dollars to your customer's purchase. In order to successfully increase a customer's order you have to provide value. That value can be as simple as an ice cold water bottle that you're selling up near the register. There are two things at play here, *benefit statements* and *consumer confidence*.

A customer will not purchase an item without a perceived value- you need a benefit statement.

Let's focus on that bottled water. It's hot outside, here's your statement.

"Wow it sure is hot outside, would you like to me to grab you one of these ice cold water bottles for the road? It's only $1." (etc.)

Your benefit statement includes the fact that the ice cold water will help against the heat outside. You also helped increase their consumer confidence by using the word "only" in your price presentation. In their mind they are processing what you said "it's only $1". Many customers will accept this offer. They know they should drink more water, it sure is hot outside and before you mentioned it they never would have thought of it. You just increased your average ticket.

Another example, a printer:

"That sure is a great printer, how about you get these replacement cartridges today as well so you know you'll have ink when you need it." Put the ink in their hands. Customer's want to avoid conflict or discomfort and will usually appreciate the suggestion that will add less hassle to them later on. Ink is a high profit item, if you can add that to the printer sale you've not only increased your average ticket, you've increased your gross margin. Great, what if they say no because there's ink in the box.

"That's true but often you'll find starter cartridges in new printers that aren't full capacity, so you might run out after 10-15 pages, I was just trying to help avoid that frustration."

This is actually a true statement, I've seen it happen, to the point a customer wanted to return the printer because they thought that was the ink capacity. I let them know the starter scenario and they asked why no one told them that before. So you've solved the average ticket goal and improved customer satisfaction. If they say no, at least you know they'll need paper to print on. Engage the customer, ask them what they are looking to print - photos, just documents, etc. You can use this info to upgrade to glossy paper for photos or grab them a case of paper if it's going to be for a big project at work.

Your turn (employee)

What do you sell the most of? What are 1-3 add-ons that make sense for that item.

Now, go sell them.

Training 2: Consumer Confidence

There are a great number of well informed customers using smart phones and ingenuity to make purchasing decisions. But just because they've read it doesn't mean they are 100% confident with their decision. You need to boost their confidence. First, make sure what they are getting is right for their needs. Ask questions that will give you more information. Sometimes a customer is caught between more than one product and will decide not to purchase any due to the difficulty in the decision. This is where you can recommend a product. Why do you recommend it? Is it a good brand? Are other customers happy with their purchase?

"I definitely understand wanting to pick the right one. I know that most of my customers go with product x and seem to be pretty happy with it."

"Well, "product x" can print 5 pages a minute, "product y "can print 12, if it were me, I'd go with "product y", I don't think you can go wrong with "product y".

Another tactic you could use to boost consumer confidence is assuming the sale. Once you've provided a benefit statement and some consumer confidence statements, start finalizing the sale, assume they're on board and move onto the next step. If it's a restaurant move forward. Let's say they were deciding on nuggets versus fries, you recommended nuggets because fries are all carbs and nuggets are high in protein (great benefit statement by the way).

So you'd say "*Okay, so did you want to get an ice cold soda with your nuggets?*"

You've assumed they have agreed with you and are now moving to your add-on.

Don't worry, they'll let you know if they haven't decided yet. Now there's an opportunity to continue to get their buy-in. One great tactic is mentioning the return period when nothing else is working.

"You know, we've got a great return policy, why don't you take it home, try it out for a few days, keep the receipt and if by this time next week it's not meeting your needs, just bring it back, find me and I'll help you exchange it for something else, sound good?"

I hate to say it, but even if it didn't meet their needs, some won't return it. But you know what, if you've really listened to their needs and recommended a product that should meet those needs, you've done your part. If you hadn't helped them they wouldn't have gotten anything and their needs really wouldn't have been met then.

Keeping your customers happy is a key in regards to repeat business and sales, but if you've sincerely made your best recommendation based on their communicated needs, don't feel bad. They could have left something out. This training is on consumer confidence.

Training 3: Asking the Right Questions

You need to ask questions and listen to your customers. The first question should be permission to assist them. *"Hi, I'm Josh, is there anything I can help you with today?"* If they don't want your help, don't linger. Stay in the area in case they need help, but move on to another customer.

If they do want your help, listen to what they say, reword the question and ask it back to them if you don't fully understand.

Customer: *"I need a thing for my phone so I can hear"*

Sales Person: *" Okay, do you mean a blue-tooth headset for your cell phone?"*

Customer: *"No, I need something for my office desk phone"*

Sales Person: *"Oh okay, let's head over to that area of the store and find what you need."*

Asking the right question can save you and the customer a lot of time.

Customer: "I'm looking for a printer."

Sales Person: "Okay, I can definitely help you with that, what are you wanting to do with your printer, print photos or mostly just documents?"

Customer: "Oh I hadn't thought of photos, that might be nice. I'll mostly be printing documents but photos would be nice as well."

Sales Person: "Alright, let's find you a printer that can do both and go over some options."

Server: "Welcome to Bob's Cafe, what can I get started for you today?"

Guest: "Well, I haven't really decided yet."

Server: "Did you want some more time to look over the menu or some help in deciding?"

Scenario 1

Guest: "Just some more time is fine"

Server: "No problem, I'll be back over in a bit, take your time"

Scenario 2

Guest: "Well, I'm trying to decide on the burger or chicken sandwich"

Server: "Do you like spicy food?"

Guest: "Not really, why?"

Server: "That's our spicy chicken sandwich"

Guest: "Oh my, okay then ,let's go with the burger."

While not all of these scenarios will match your needs, you should be able to get the picture.

Don't ask yes or no questions, get to the heart of what they need as quickly as you can.

Training 4: Gross Margin

Gross margin won't translate over to your customer, but it's the most important part of your sales business. If you sell $1,000,000 in product and make no profit, you're out of business. That's it, game over. If you sell $10,000 in product and make $9,000 profit, you're doing the right thing. Now these are exaggerated scenarios but you get the picture, you're here to make money.

Your staff needs to know what makes your business money, what keeps the lights on?

In most electronics stores, it's ink. Ink in some sales locations can easily represent a 60% profit per sale. So any easy training for your employee is to have the observe where customers are in the store and reach out to them even more if they are in a high gross margin area. In my store, if a customer was at the ink wall, so was a sales person. If they were in furniture the same applied as at my store furniture typically had a 40% profit margin.

If it's a restaurant, your quick serve high gross margin items are typically drinks and fried foods. They require very little labor and produce a nice return on profits. Train your servers to recommend fries or add-on drinks to orders.

Find out what your high profit items are, don't assume, run a report or reach out to someone who can. A nifty trick is to visibly mark a pricing label with a pen mark or dot. Teach your sales staff that dotted items have a high gross margin and if possible should be something considered when making a recommendation. By training them to simply look for the mark, you can improve your gross margin.

Cashiers are the last chance for a gross margin and average ticket boost. Why do we care about average ticket? For the most part increased sales can also mean increased gross margin. If someone buys a notepad for $2 and you add on a pack of pens for $1, you boosted your average ticket to $3. If the notepad had a $1 gross margin profit, and the pens had a $.50 gross margin profit, now you took what would have been $1 of profit and turned it into $1.50. Not much, but that's a 50% increase in your gross margin for that sale, THAT IS A BIG DEAL. Now take that across the board and you're seeing nothing like you've ever seen before. Your boss's boss is going to take notice and visit your store and ask what you're doing differently. Trust me, that's what happened to me. I had a national executive request to specifically visit my store while they were in our state because of our results in a category.

Know your high gross margin items, make them easily recognized by your staff, and train them to recommend and sell them and you will see increased profits, and likely a bonus if your pay is based on performance metrics.

Cashiers

Cashiers are your greatest average ticket and gross margin employees. Don't just throw a low level employee on the register. Put a sales person on the register. You can rotate who's on the register if needed, but don't neglect this vital spot.

Not every sales person will engage with every customer, but every customer has to check out, so they will at one point end up at the register. Have a great sales person here. Make them on the top of your priority list for training, you won't regret it.

Closing

The final recommendation I can make is to never lose sight of why you are there. If you're the sales manager or supervisor, that is your job. Other functions may overlap, you may find yourself on a register, or making copies, or hiring. All of these are part of your job, but your main focus should remain on sales. Train one person and let them repeat that training to others. One-on-One produces the best results from my years of experience in sales and food service. Don't waste valuable sales time on pointless training. Keep training short- five minutes is ideal. Have team huddles at the start of a shift, clearly communicate your goals for that day, that week, and beyond. Also lead by example. Make it a point that no matter how busy you are with other things, that you take time to help at least one customer per day. You can boost those sales and profits yourself with 30 customers per month. Your team will see you do it and they will follow in your example.

www.ingramcontent.com/pod-product-compliance
Lightning Source LLC
Chambersburg PA
CBHW070430190526
45169CB00003B/1489